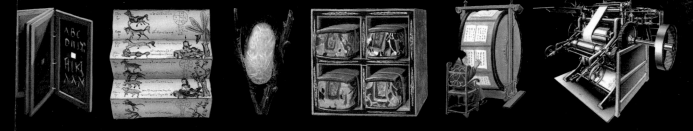

The History of Making Books

Contents

★   ★   ★

You can find more information about names and
words marked with an * beginning on page 33.
This shape, ❑, shows you where a sticker goes.

Ancient Writing

Powdered pigment

The word **book** comes from the Old English *boc* or "written sheet." But people wrote down their ideas and stories long

Mortar

before there were books as we know them today. Thousands of years ago in Mesopotamia*, people recorded everything from laws to literature on clay tablets. The ancient Egyptian **scribes*** used about 700 hieroglyphs or picture **characters*** to write tributes to the pharaoh or moral advice on

Egyptian inkwell and writing instruments

papyrus* rolls. In the fourth century B.C., Greeks and Romans also used papyrus rolls, which could be up to 50 feet long!

The Library* of Alexandria in Egypt was formed ca. 300 B.C. Scientists and scholars used the more than 500,000 papyrus rolls stored the

An ancient Roman wood-and-wax codex*, third century A.D. ❑ ►

Baked Like Bread

The Mesopotamians living in the Tigris and Euphrates River Valleys molded damp clay into tablets. They used a stylus* to cut in cuneiforms*, or wedge-shaped writing symbols. Then they let the tablets dry in the sun or baked them in ovens. The hard tablets were stored side by side on shelves, often in temples.

Scribe's tools: inkwell, papyrus box, and stylus ❑

Wax, Wood, and Papyrus

Ancient Greeks and Romans kept written records on wax-covered wooden tablets. Sometimes several tablets would be hinged together with leather or metal. Romans called this a codex. The construction was an early form of what we now call a book.

Scrolls in a Jar

Ancient Egyptians wrote on papyrus sheets that were pasted together to make long scrolls*. To protect the scrolls from water or insect damage, the Egyptians often stored them in wood or clay jars filled with cedar oil.

The Torah is a sacred Jewish work that contains the first five books of the Bible's Old Testament. In Hebrew, the word means "teaching" or "law."

A mosaic or tile picture of the famous Roman poet Virgil (70–19 B.C.) holding a scroll called a volumen ►

Asian Ingenuity

Chinese silk scroll, fifth century A.D.

Silk fabric is m[ade]
from the fibers [a]
silkworm produ[ces]
to form its coco[on.]
Silk is supple an[d]
can be folded or
rolled.

Like the Mesopotamians with their clay and the Egyptians with their papyrus, people in Asian countries used the materials around them to preserve their ideas. Texts were handwritten on birch bark, palm leaves, bamboo stems, and silk. The Chinese are credited with creating **paper** earlier than the second century A.D. They also developed **printing*** techniques ca. A.D. 500, centuries before the Europeans.

Japan was heavily influenced by Chinese learning and culture. By around A.D. 900, the Japanese had invented a way to write their words using Chinese-style characters.

Part of a Chinese bamboo book. These heavy objects remained in use until about the third century A.D.

An accordion book printed in China, 17th century. Its cover is made of scented wood and silk brocade.

Bamboo

Bamboo was plentiful in ancient China. When it was cut, dried, and polished, it made a good writing surface. The bamboo slats were tied together with leather or silk cords. Chinese writers used brushes and ink and wrote in vertical columns. They read their bamboo books from top to bottom and from right to left.

Silk

In the fourth century B.C., Chinese authors began to write with brushes on pieces of silk several yards long. To make these beautiful silk scrolls easier to store and to read, they were rolled onto a baton.

Paper

The Chinese pasted together sheets of paper to make scrolls. They also folded paper back and forth to make what is now called an accordion book, because the folds resemble the bellows of that musical instrument. By the fifth century A.D., most Chinese writers used only paper.

In Tibet, a region in southwest China, many books were written on long, horizontal sheets of paper, after the style of the Indian *pothi* described on the overlay.

Arabian Treasures

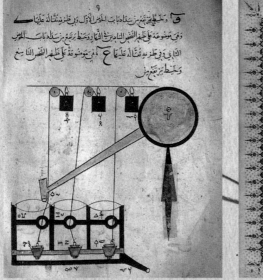

Calligrapher*

The **Islamic** Arab Empire flourished from the 7th to the 12th centuries A.D. It extended from Spain to Persia, which is now called Iran. Papermaking had been introduced by Chinese captured in Arab conquests, and cities such as Baghdad and Damascus became great centers of book production. The **literacy** rate was very high; about one in five **Arabs** could **read***. Muslim **scholars** produced beautiful books on religion, poetry, mathematics, medicine, astrology, engineering, and other arts and sciences.

A treatise on mechanics, 14th century

A Koran, sometimes spelled Qur'ān, 17th century

From India...

In India, palm tree leaves were used to make book pages, called *pothi*. The largest part of the leaf was cooked in milk, dried, and polished with a shell.

dian writers inscribed the *pothi* using a metal stylus. Then they rubbed the pages with colored ink, which filled the grooves or arks left by the stylus. This made their writing easier to see.

...to Thailand

Accordion books*, like this horizontal one, could also be found in Thailand in Southeast Asia.

On the Indonesian island of Sumatra, people used books made from folded bark. These bark books opened vertically and were re[ad] horizontally from left to right.

◀ A Koran case, inlaid with mother-of-pearl □

Koran

The holiest book an Arab writer could produce was the Koran, a transcription of the words of the Islamic God, Allah, to the Muslim prophet Muhammad. It was mostly compiled after the prophet's death in A.D. 632. A Muslim caliph, or regional ruler, worried that these important teachings would be lost if they were not recorded and assembled into one text. He ordered that all of Muhammad's followers who had memorized or written down the sayings be interviewed. By around 651, there was an official version of the Koran that could be reproduced by copyists. They used a beautiful form of handwriting called calligraphy, which was read from right to left, and they decorated pages with borders and backgrounds. These decorations, called arabesques, were an important part of all Arabian design.

From Greek to Arabic

Islamic copyists also translated and wrote down the works of Aristotle (384–322 B.C.). Western copyists later heavily depended upon these books in Arabic for information about the famous Greek philosopher.

Poetry

"A loaf of bread, a jug of wine — and thou," is the well-known, though inexact, translation of a line from the *Rubáiyát,* by one of Persia's most famous medieval poets, Omar Khayyám. Poetry books were highly valued in the royal courts.

The shape in the background sketched in red is from a 12th-century book of mathematics.

Book of Wonders, 14th century

7

Parchment

1. Parchment makers of the Middle Ages
2. Use the sticker in the back pocket of the book to take a microscopic look at sheepskin parchment. ❐

For more than 2,000 years, people in Africa, Europe, Asia, and the Americas wrote stories on **leather** or used animal **hides** to make book pages. Around the second century B.C., people in Asia Minor began to process sheep and goat hides to produce what is called **parchment**. First the hides were soaked in water. Then they were covered with lime and scraped to remove the animal hair. Next the damp hides were stretched on a wooden **frame** and left to dry in the sun. Some were **bleached** with chalk or with lime. It took 12 sheepskins to make a book with 150 pages.

By the 16th century, most bookmakers used paper, but parchment was still used for special books and other things. That's why college diplomas once were called sheepskins!

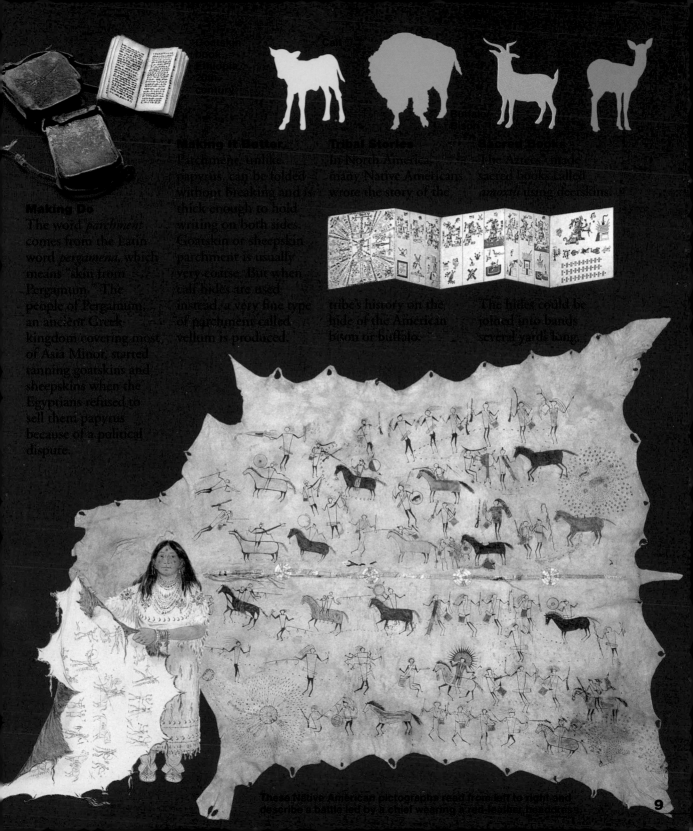

Making Do

The word *parchment* comes from the Latin word *pergamena*, which means "skin from Pergamum." The people of Pergamum, an ancient Greek kingdom covering most of Asia Minor, started tanning goatskins and sheepskins when the Egyptians refused to sell them papyrus because of a political dispute.

Making It Better

Parchment, unlike papyrus, can be folded without breaking and is thick enough to hold writing on both sides. Goatskin or sheepskin parchment is usually very coarse. But when calf hides are used instead, a very fine type of parchment called vellum is produced.

Tribal Stories

In North America, many Native Americans wrote the story of the tribe's history on the hide of the American bison or buffalo.

Sacred Books

The Aztecs made sacred books called *amoxtli* using deerskins. The hides could be joined into bands several yards long.

These Native American pictographs read from left to right and describe a battle led by a chief wearing a red feather headdress.

Illuminated Manuscripts

1. An illuminated capital *P* from an Italian Bible, 12th century
2. A page from a Spanish commentary on the Bible, 10th century

After the fall of the Roman Empire in the fifth century, much of Europe was troubled by war and invasions. But in the peace and quiet of European **monasteries**, monks of the Middle Ages (ca. A.D. 476–1453) copied the texts that preserved important parts of Western religion, culture, and history. Their beautifully decorated, or **illuminated**, **manuscripts***** were made from folded sheets of vellum or other parchment and bound into covers. Church leaders discouraged the use of scrolls and of paper, which were thought to be pagan or un-Christian.

The scholar Saint Jerome (ca. A.D. 340–420) in his scriptorium. He was a translator of the Bible and is shown here with a lion, which, according to legend, he rescued in a desert in Syria.

Paper

The Chinese began experimenting with **paper** perhaps as early as the second century B.C. They soaked straw, tree bark, fishnets,

¹ and plants such as mulberry, hemp, or bamboo in water, then pounded them into **pulp**. The pulp was poured over a **screen** to let the water drain. When it dried, there was a piece of paper! The

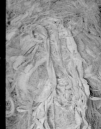

use of paper spread at first slowly through the West. There was just not much demand for it. Most Europeans at the time could not read. And in many parts of medieval Europe, anything written on paper had no legal standing or value.

An early European paper mill. The first paper mill in the United States opened in Roxboro, Pennsylvania, in 1690.

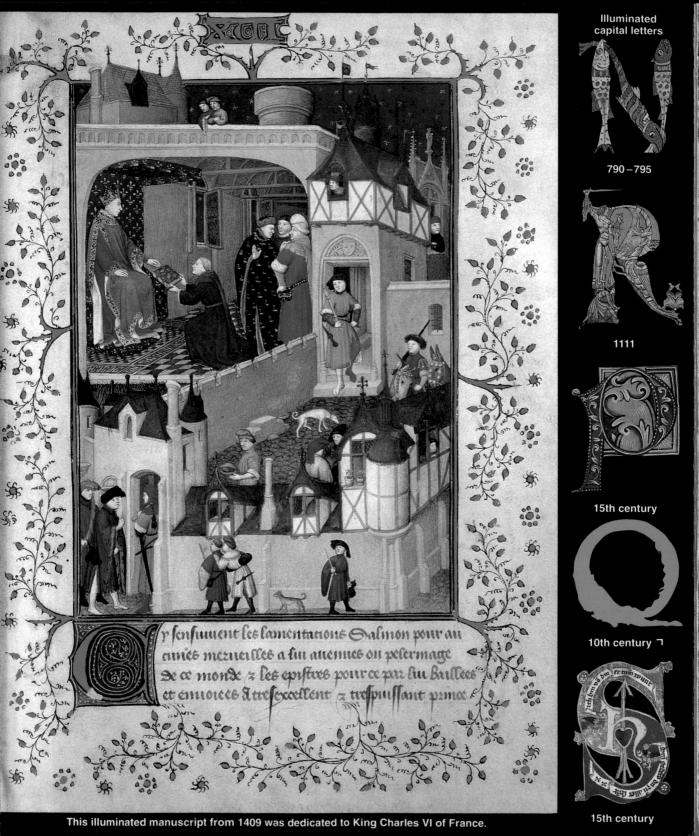

790 – 795

1111

15th century

10th century

15th century

This illuminated manuscript from 1409 was dedicated to King Charles VI of France.

1

1. A monk rules the lines that will serve as a guide for his writing.
2. French Bible, ca. 1350
3. Latin Book of Prayers, ca. 790–795

2

3

Scriptorium

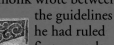 Scribes worked in the monastery's scriptorium, a large room with wooden desks and chairs. The top of their writing desks or lecterns were sharply angled to hold manuscript pages almost upright.

From about A.D. 1200, independent scribes—both men and women—began producing manuscript books in studios near universities.

Ssssssh!

The scribes toiled in silence during the daylight hours. They did not have candles or lamps, because it was too risky to have any fire near their precious manuscripts.

Monks at Work

Monks manufactured books from the preparation of the parchment to the binding of the pages. They created some manuscripts from dictation and others by copying religious or classical texts.

Page by Page

A monk wrote between the guidelines he had ruled first on each page. Then his manuscript was proofread* or checked for errors, before going to another scribe who put in titles or chapter heads, often in red or blue. After that, the illuminator added beautiful illustrations and decorative letters. Then the pages were sewn together and laced into a wood-and-leather cover.

filings, oak bark, and gallnuts to make black ink. To mix red ink, they used ground cinnabar, an expensive ore.

Tools of the Trade

Monks wrote with quill pens and sometimes used hard or lead points to draw guidelines. They boiled iron

The lectern sometimes had a smaller shelf on top to hold the work being copied.

Stone for sharpening knives with which to cut quill pens

Hard points for ruling lines on sheets of parchment or vellum

Detail of a dragon from the French manuscript *Apocalypse de Saint-Sever*, 11th-century ▶

Brightly colored manuscript ink came from plants or insects: (a) dyer's rocket plant = yellow; (b) indigo plant or (c) woad plant = blue; (d) dried bodies of scale insects called kermes = red. ▢

Illuminating an initial:
1. The illuminator traced the outlines with a very fine feather pen and diluted ink.
2. He applied gold powder or gold leaf over a layer of egg white.

3. The outlines of the colors were traced with the feather pen, then filled in with a fine, animal-hair brush.
4. Finally, delicate strokes of white and the highlights were added.

Familiar Monsters

Although monks were Christians, many of the subjects of their illuminations, such as dragons, devils, and other beasts, were inspired by figures from ancient religions or myths.

a

b

c

d

1

2

3

4

Decorated initials could be abstract designs or pictures of people, animals, or scenes.

Pine trees are cut up to make pulp for modern paper.

This papermaking machine, patented by John Gamble in England in 1803, could produce a continuous sheet of paper over 30 feet long.

Early Paper Mills

The paper mill on the facing page shows how paper was made in Europe from the 12th century. Flowing water turned the wheel, which turned mallets in the vat to pound the pulp. A mold was dipped in and out of the liquid pulp and was shaken. The shaking action fused the fibers together to form sheets of paper. These sheets were layered in piles between pieces of felt and put into a press to squeeze out all the water. Then they were hung up to dry. It was time-consuming work, but paper eventually replaced parchment because it was much cheaper to produce.

Watermarks

Around 1270, Italian papermakers created watermarks by twisting wire into simple designs and attaching them to the bottom of the paper mold. The designs were identifying marks that could be seen if you held up the sheet to the light. Watermarks might also be decorative like this 1587 elephant watermark from Germany.

From Rags to Wood

Over time, papermaking changed. Machines that sped up the process were introduced in France in 1798 and in England in 1803, making paper cheaper and more plentiful. By 1850, wood pulp paper began to replace rag pulp paper. Wood pulp is still used today, and modern machines can make long bands or webs of paper on continually moving belts and rollers.

Modern papermaking machines heat the pulp, then press, drain, dry, and smooth it into paper in a continuous motion.

Printing

As early as the sixth century A.D., the Chinese and Japanese **engraved** or cut words and images into **wood blocks**, then inked them and pressed the blocks against a writing surface like paper or silk. Texts could be reproduced many times this way. By the 11th century, the Chinese were using one-character **blocks**, the first movable type. By the 1300s, Europeans were also printing from wood blocks. Then in 1438, **Johannes Gutenberg** helped revolutionize printing — with his jewelers' tools and a wine press.

As a goldsmith in Mainz, Germany, Gutenberg had engraving tools and metal molds that would help him create movable ty

Pages were checked for the quality of their images. It took a great deal of strength to pull the press bar each time a sheet was printed.

1. This coinmaker is using a punch, a tool that inspired Gutenberg.
2. The punch leaves its imprint in the copper. ⌐

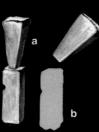

a

b

Metal characters were cast one by one in molds. ▼
◄ After the pieces of type were taken from the mold (a), extra bits of metal that were produced as part of the casting process, called jets, needed to be broken off so that each piece of type would be the same height (b). ⌐

1

Making the Type

Because thousands of characters or pieces of type were needed to print a book, Gutenberg needed to

2

find a way to make them in great quantity. He did this by carving a letter backward on the end of a hard metal rod called a punch. Then he drove the punch into a small

plate of softer metal. The punch left an impression of the letter that read in the right direction. This character impression became the matrix. The matrix was then fitted inside a type mold, into which a liquid metal —usually a mixture of lead, tin, and antimony*— was poured. The molten metal immediately hardened inside the type mold, forming a piece of type.

Too Big? Too Small?

No matter what character was cast, it had to be the same height as all of the printer's other type. That way, all the characters would form a flat printing surface and the platen, or plate, would impress them evenly against the paper. Early printers filed the type to make it uniform.

Roll the Presses!

Other European craftsmen were experimenting like Gutenberg, and hundreds of presses were in operation across Europe by the end of the 1400s. A printer could now produce in a day what a scribe took months to accom-

plish. In less than 50 years, the number of books in Europe jumped from less than 30,000 to more than 9 million. The Puritans set up a printing press in Cambridge, Massachusetts, in 1638.

Jean-Antoine Laurent, *Gutenberg Inventing the Printing Press*, 1830

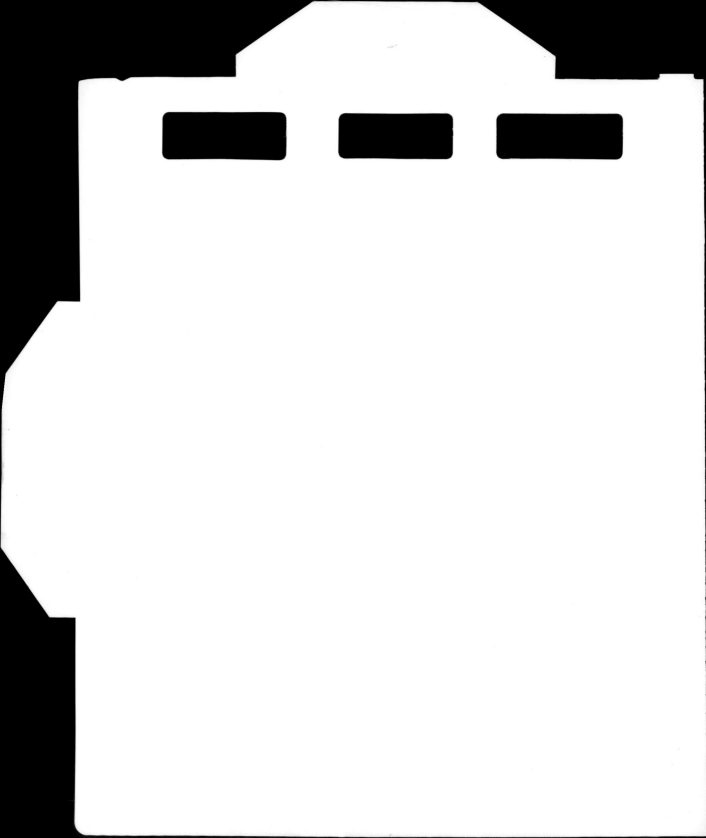

Boxed Type

Printers kept their metal type in wooden type cases. The cases were divided into compartments, one for each

letter. The size of the compartment depended on how frequently that letter appeared in the language being set. In English, the letter *e* had the biggest compartment.

Letter by Letter

Type was set by arranging the letters upside down and backward in a line on the composing stick.

Word by Word

Blank pieces of metal were used to separate words and lines. These blank spacings would not print because they were lower than the raised type letters.

New Type

Printers and typographers were constantly creating new typefaces* or fonts*. They experimented with size, proportion, and design to make their work more beautiful and legible.

How-to Books

Type was made and set by hand for almost four centuries. There were books that explained how to properly set type and how to make a book's design enhance and complement the subject matter.

Famous Faces

Some designers and their fonts became very well known. In 15th-century Venice, Aldus Manutius* created a very legible, straight letter or roman font that other Europeans

Printing form▼

used as a model for more than 250 years. He was also the first printer to produce slanting or italic letters.

Printing Machines

a

b

c

◄ These capital *A*'s show three printing techniques: (a) letterpress, (b) engraved, and (c) lithographic.

Printers' ink is very thick and heavy. ►

The 19th century was an age of great invention, especially for power-driven machines. Printers used steam engines to build **printing presses** that could produce more books than ever, faster than ever. Advances in photography allowed printers to make **photographic plates** that were easier to use than handset metal characters. With literacy on the rise, people wanted books! **Publishers*** began to heavily advertise their titles, especially novels, which became **best-sellers**.

Paper was placed sheet by sheet under the printing rollers. Press workers checked the quality of the printed pages carefully.

A Stanhope press, 1795, a platen press, where the printing surface and press are both flat

A Marinoni press, ca. 1845, a flat-bed cylinder press, where the printing surface is flat and the press is cylindrical

A photogravure press, ca. 1910, where the printing surface and press are both cylindrical

Iron and Levers

Around 1805, Charles Stanhope, Third Earl of Chesterfield (1753–1816), modified the printing press in England. Most presses of the time were wooden, hand operated, and roughly based on Gutenberg's design. Stanhope's press was made from iron. He used levers instead of the large screw to force the plate down. This meant less effort for the press worker and a cleaner imprint on the paper.

Keys and Punches

The Linotype machine (1886) made it possible to set type automatic-ally. When you type on its keyboard, it produces a perforated, or punched, band of paper. This band is decoded by the caster, the machine that casts the type in hot metal. If you make a single-character mistake, you have to recast the whole line.

The Monotype machine (1889) operates on the same principle, but each character was cast individually, so it was easier to correct any errors.

Steam and Wheels

The Koenig press (ca. 1812) used a steam engine and wheels to print almost four times faster than any hand-operated press could.

On a Roll

Incorporating cylinders into printing presses made them more productive. The constantly turning rollers made it possible to increase printing speeds to produce more books. Offset lithography, one of the most widely used printing processes today, has two rollers and a cylindrical plate. However, new advances in computer technology are creating new ways to print, using electronic signals rather than presses.

a

b

A Monotype machine has (a) a keyboard and (b) a caster.

...pe was originally composed or put ...gether by hand. Some really ...illed composers could assemble ...early 2,000 characters in an hour. ... Monotype operator could probably do 6,000 ...aracters in the same amount of time. Today's ...omputers can set 1,000 characters in a second.

19

Colorful Books

Modern **color separation** has made printing in color easy. This four-color printing process is based on the idea that all colors are a combination of primary colors. A computerized **scanner** uses an electronic "eye" to separate an image into the three primary colors plus black. It reproduces this information as **dots** on transparent films. These films are used to make four printing plates that go on **cylinders**. After the paper has gone through all the cylinders, you have the complete color of the original image.

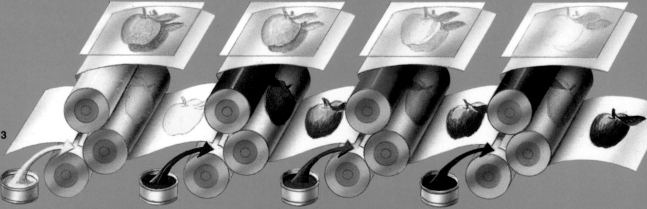

1. The dot screen: Dots are larger or smaller according to the density of the color to be reproduced.
2. A loupe is the small magnifying glass a printer uses to check the dot-screen pattern.
3. The paper goes through the cylinders of an offset press and receives a different-colored ink on each set of rollers.

Yellow film

Magenta film

Cyan film

Black film

se the stickers in the back pocket of the book to color in this apple.

The three primary colors — yellow, magenta (a type of red), and cyan (a type of blue) — can make a whole rainbow of colors. Black is used to produce outlines and detail. Printers can adjust the percentage of colors used so that the picture will print realistically.

Bookbinding

Gold or goatskin. Precious jewels or paper. Leather or velvet. All kinds of materials have been used to **bind** a book between its cover. After parchment or paper sheets were folded and stitched together, they needed a covering to protect them from curling and other damage. Around the fifth century A.D., bookmakers began to lace their manuscripts into wooden **boards**, which they would then cover with **leather**. Until the early 1800s, the majority of books were bound in this way.

Gold-and-precious-stones cover, ca. 1200

Velvet-and-engraved-metal cover, ca. 1480

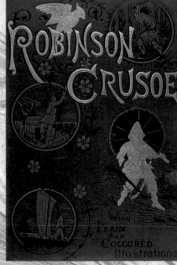

Leather cover, decorated with gold, 19th century

Illustrations of marine life from a natural history book, 1753

Illustrations of surgeons' tools from a medical dictionary of surgery, 1743

By the late 16th century, the spread of printing had greatly increased the availability of books all over Europe. Cities such as Paris, France, Venice, Italy, and Frankfurt am Main, Germany, became major publishing centers. One of the world's biggest book fairs is still held in Frankfurt. More books allowed for a new **exchange** of knowledge and ideas. But the **contents** of books, and who had the right or privilege to print them, was strictly **controlled** by the church or the state.

Booksellers printed new versions of ancient classics, or Bibles or religious works. If a book had an author, he was usually paid with copies of his book. Taking money from a publisher was frowned upon until the mid-1700s.

A book about medicine, 1493

A zoology book, 16th century

Denis Diderot's *Encyclopédie*, 1751–17

A burnisher is a long-handled tool with an agate or smooth piece of quartz at the end, used to add gilt to the page edges.

Binding by Hand

After the paper or parchment sheets were folded into signatures* to make a book, the bookbinder pasted down the endpapers at the front and the back of the signatures. Then the signatures were placed on a sewing frame and stitched together. The boards used for the cover were laced on and the spine was rounded with a hammer. Then the whole thing was covered with leather. After the leather was polished, the covered book was put into a binding press.

Finishing

Decorating the cover is called finishing. This could mean stamping a thin layer of gold onto the leather.

The parts of a book:
(a) spine
(b) top edge
(c) fore-edge
(d) upper cover

Hardcover Books

Most books today are bound by machine. After a book has been printed in sheets with multiples of four pages on them, a folding machine folds the sheets into signatures. A mechanic assembler puts all the folded signatures together, then sends them along to the stitcher. When the pages are all stitched together, they form a spine, which is rounded and coated with paste. A giant blade trims the book to size and the book is ready to be covered. Modern hardcover books have very stiff cardboard bindings, which are usually covered with cloth.

Paperbacks

Paperbacks have flexible covers. Their folded signatures are not sewn together. The spine is coated with paste, and the cover gets pressed on.

Become a bookbinder, using the stickers in the back pocket of the book. ❐

This book from 1512 has the name and a portrait of its author, Angel Politien, on the fore-edge.

◄ *The History of Making Books* has a concealed spiral binding.

Hawker* of books

Italian philosopher and writer Giordano Bruno (1548–1600) was burned alive in Rome in 1600. His writings and his support of Nicolaus Copernicus's theory of the universe outraged church authorities.

During the Spanish civil war (1936–1939), banned books were burned in Barcelona. ▼

Banned Books

Church and state were tightly intertwined in Europe from the 14th to the 16th centuries. To prevent any questioning of their authority or rulings, religious

Power of the P

The 17th cen[...] greater dem[...] books that [...] on law,

Burning Ideas

A Chinese emperor had all books that weren't "useful" burned in 213 B.C. The Virginia Colony did not allow any printing in the 1680s. The Nazis burned books they

thought were dangerous or decadent in the 1930s and 1940s. Censors want to suppress ideas with which they don't agree. This issue is becoming more complicated as books and other materials become easily available through electronic transmission.

and governmen[...] officials establ[...] censorship* After exam[...] censors [...] refused[...] to pu[...]

Auto-da-fé, or destruction of an object by fire, means an "act of faith" in Portuguese.

At the Library

1. In the Middle Ages, books were displayed on shelves or were stored flat. ❏
2. Tibetan monks kept their books in a divided box, with a colored niche for each book.

Ancient Egyptians could consult papyrus rolls in a **palace** library at Thebes, whose doorway was engraved with the words MEDICINE OF THE SOUL. Hebrew scholars could consult the now famous Dead Sea Scrolls in a library in Palestine in the first century A.D. Many European libraries of the Middle Ages were housed in churches or **monasteries**. Other medieval book collections were established along with the growing numbers of **universities**. By the late 1800s, **public libraries**, where most people could look at and borrow materials, opened in all parts of the world. Today, many libraries are connected electronically.

3. This ancient wheel allowed Chinese readers to consult several books at a time.
4. Books were so precious in the Middle Ages, they were sometimes chained to the desk to prevent theft.

IGENES
GR. LAT.

TOM. 1.

ORIGENES
GR. LAT.

TOM. 2.

VAILLANT
NUMISMATA

OE
SPI

uilt in the 14th and 15th centuri
longer all be stored flat or on

1. Tarzan of the Apes, written by Edgar Rice Burroughs ... book
Illustrated by Burne Hogarth, was published in 1914. ... book
2. The Story of Babar, written and illustrated by ... s them.
Jean de Brunhoff, appeared in 1931. ◻

For centuries, children have loved books of **folktales** and other stories. But books published specifically for children did not really become popular until the early 19th century. There were no **children's bookstores** in the United States until one opened in Boston in 1916. Now some companies publish only children's books. One popular type of children's publishing is **picture books**, where beautiful art adds to the story.

...servation

...ve
... teams that
... repair
... books. They
...cal processes
...t books or
... paper to
... pages.
...es a library
... lend an old or
... book, but you
...uest permission
... at it. If an
...tant book is
...d saving, it will
...otographed, page-
...age, so that at least
...simile of the book
...ins.

Little Red Riding Hood, written by Charles Perrault in 1695, was illustrated by Gustave Doré in the 19th century.

...lights helps keep the ... temple library in Korea

28

Carlo Collodi's *Pinocchio*, illus. by Attilio Mussino, 1935

WHERE THE WILD THINGS ARE

STORY AND PICTURES BY MAURICE SENDAK

Maurice Sendak's *Where the Wild Things Are*, 1963

Alice's Adventures in Wonderland, illus. by A. Rackham, 1907

Antoine de Saint-Exupéry's *The Little Prince*, 1943

Words to Know

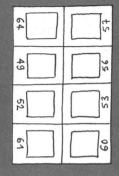

A bookmobile or library on wheels

Accordion Book

A method of book page folding invented by the Chinese. Pages were folded back and forth, somewhat like the bellows section of the musical instrument the accordion. A thicker page was sometimes added to cover the accordion pages to prevent the book from unfolding.

Antimony

A metallic element that, when blended in with other metals, increases their hardness. Antimony, which can be hard, lustrous, and silvery white, was used by Johannes Gutenberg and other typefounders to make metal type that could withstand the pressure of the press without breaking.

Author

A writer of literary works. Until the 17th century, an author did not own his works and a publisher was free to reproduce those works however and whenever he wanted. In the 18th century, European and American laws began to be written to protect the rights of the author. These laws of literary ownership are known as copyright. Today, the author usually holds the copyright or the ownership of the right to publish and distribute a work.

Aztec

An Indian people of ancient North America, who lived in parts of what is now Mexico. Their highly developed civilization flourished in the 15th century, before most of it was destroyed in the 1520s by the army

How an eight-page signature is folded into the correct page order

of the Spanish invader, Hernán Cortés.

Bookseller

A person who sells books. In the early centuries of book production, the bookseller, the printer, and the publisher were often the same person. At first, a bookseller would sell only the output from his own press, which in the 15th century might be at most 200 copies of any one book. But as the demand for books increased, booksellers began to exchange books with other printers and booksellers to increase the number of books each had for sale.

Books in the Middle Ages were protected by bars.

the Arab Empire as well as in China and Japan, where it still flourishes today. In the West, it is often used for formal invitations, notices, and official documents. This type of penmanship is very painstaking, and requires careful skill in using a pen or brush.

CD-ROM

Compact discs with read-only memory. These optical discs are used to store digital texts, images, and sounds. Digitilization translates information into a binary code, or a number series of zeros and ones that the computer reads and translates. Many books, especially reference books, are now produced as CD-ROMs, which can hold up to 250,000 pages and 7,000 nonmoving images.

Censorship

The efforts of a government, religious body, or any other group to control information.

The Chinese character *ts'e*, which means "list"

This eventually lead to the division of printing, publishing, and bookselling into separate industries.

Calligrapher

A person who practices calligraphy, or the art of beautiful handwriting. Calligraphy is an ancient art and was practiced in

In the Middle Ages, books were laid flat on shelves.

Throughout history, printed materials have always been subject to one form of censorship or

A Chinese bookseller

another. Today, new forms of electronic communication are making information more available than at any other time in history, causing policy makers to struggle with new questions about censorship.

Characters

Written or printed symbols or marks used to convey information. Characters can be hieroglyphs, letters, numerals, or punctuation marks.

Codex

Texts written on pages bound together side by side. A codex is another name for what we today call a book. After about the fourth century A.D., codices began to replace the scroll, as they were easier to store and to handle.

Colophon

A colophon is the inscription that appears at the end of a book. A colophon often includes the names of the editor, the designer, the typeface and typesetter, the printer, the type of paper the book is printed on, and the medium of any artwork in the book. In the Middle Ages, a colophon sometimes contained information about the patron who had paid for a manuscript's production. The first printed books had colophons similar to those found in manuscripts. But by the early 16th century, the colophon was largely replaced by the title page, which appears at the front of the book.

Cuneiforms

The wedge-shaped characters that ancient Mesopotamian peoples, such as the Assyrians or the Persians, used in their writings.

Font

A set of type that includes letters, numerals, and punctuation marks, which are all related by design.

Format

During the first 350 years of printing, when paper was made by hand in paper molds, a book's size was determined in part by the size of the sheets of paper on which it was printed. But size was also determined by a book's format, or, how

A chained book

many times the sheet had been folded to make the book's pages. For example, the format of a book made up of sheets of paper folded once is

called a folio. And the format of a book whose sheets have been folded twice, into quarters, is called a quarto. If the book is made up of sheets folded three times, it's an octavo.

Hawker
A traveling seller of engravings, gazettes, calendars, and small books, as opposed to a bookseller with a shop.

Library
A collection of manuscripts or printed materials. The earliest known libraries were in China and date back to ca. 1767 B.C. Although there were many Greek and Roman libraries, none

survived the fall of the Roman Empire in the fifth century A.D. The most famous library in ancient times was the Library of Alexandria, which contained hundreds of thousands of scrolls.
The first European libraries appeared in the late A.D. 700s.
The word *library* comes from the Latin *libraria*, meaning "bookseller's shop."

Manuscript
A text written by hand, from the Latin words *manus*, meaning "hand," and *scribere*, meaning "to write." Use of this word has changed as printing technology changed. Editors and

publishers now use the word *manuscript* to mean an author's work before it is published in print or electronic form.

Mesopotamia
The ancient country of Southwest Asia that lay between the Tigris and Euphrates Rivers, in what is now Iraq. Its fertility favored the development of a great civilization.

Papyrus
A tall water plant, which was especially plentiful on the banks of the Nile River in Egypt. Its stem was cut into strips, which were then beaten, dried, pasted, and used by ancient peoples as a writing surface.

Some booksellers sold their wares in the streets.

Pocketbooks

In 1501, Italian printer and publisher Aldus Manutius made a set of Latin books sized small to fit in a pouch for easy distribution.

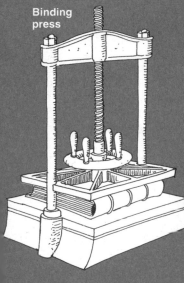

Binding press

Other printers followed his example. Because of their size, these "pocketbooks" were easy for book hawkers to carry—or conceal if they happened to be secretly selling a banned book. Small pocketbooks or paperbacks were introduced to U.S. readers in the 19th century, but did not really take off until the 20th century. Paperbacks are now usually manufactured in great quantity, using inexpensive materials. They are sold everywhere from bookstores to supermarkets, newsstands, airports, and train stations, at a lower price than hardcover books.

Printing

The reproduction of inked text or images, using a variety of techniques and materials. From the mid-15th century until the early 19th century, printing was done by hand on wooden printing presses. But since the early 1800s, many new mechanical and recently, electronic, methods have been used.

Proofreader

A person who reads a text to check it for accuracy in spelling, grammar, and other fine points of typography and design.

Publisher

A person or company that produces books. Today, publishers employ an editorial and design staff to develop and acquire books and make arrangements with authors and illustrators to publish their works. They also hire typesetters, printers, and binders to manufacture the books. Then the publishers' marketing staff help generate interest in the books with advertising, while the sales staff or outside distributors get the books to bookstores and customers. In the early centuries of printing, a publisher was often also a printer and a bookseller.

Reading

Language and culture influence how words are recorded, whether they be on a scroll, on a page, or on any other printed or electronic medium. That, in turn, determines how texts are read and understood. In Western countries, materials are

An ancient Roman library

generally read from left to right, starting at the top and ending at the bottom of a text. Books written in

An accordion book

Arabic and Hebrew are read right to left. In Chinese and Japanese books, texts in columns are read from top to bottom and from right to left. There are also specialized printing and reading systems such as Braille. Developed in the 19th century and named after its inventor, Louis Braille, Braille is a reading system for the blind or visually impaired. It uses an alphabet of raised dots to represent letters. Braille books are read by running your fingers over the pages.

Recto/Verso
The two sides of a sheet of paper, or the two pages of a spread in a book. The recto is the front side or the right-hand page of a book.

The verso is the back or the left-hand page of a book.

Scribe
A person who wrote manuscripts by hand or copied existing texts the same way. Scribes were responsible for book production before there were printing presses.

Scrolls
Rolled papyrus, parchment, or paper manuscripts.

Signature
A folded press sheet with printed pages on both sides. The pages of the book are arranged in such a way that when the sheet is folded in half again and again, all the folded pages are in the proper order. A signature may consist of 8, 16, 24, 32, or 64 pages. *See* the drawing on page 37.

Stylus
A sharp-pointed writing instrument. It was used by Mesopotamian peoples and Egyptians, among others.

Title Page
Manuscripts and most of the first printed books had colophons, but no

title pages. The first lines of the text identified the work. The title page replaced the colophon by the early 1500s in Europe. It usually includes the title and author of the work, the printer, the publisher, and the date and city of publication.

Typeface
With metal characters, the part that prints or makes the impression. Typeface is also used to mean the style or design of these characters. Thousands of typefaces are currently in use, and type designers use computers to create new ones all the time.

Type Foundry
A workshop or factory where metal typefaces were designed and manufactured.

Index

Time Line

	Prehistory/Antiquity 2 million B.C.–A.D. 476	**Middle Ages** A.D. 476–1453	**Renaissance** 1453–1600
Books	**ca. 2500 B.C.** Egyptians discover use of papyrus as writing material **669–630 B.C.** King Ashurbanipal of Assyria assembles collection of cuneiform texts at Nineveh **ca. 300 B.C.** The Library of Alexandria founded **A.D. 105** Ts'ai Lun invents paper in China	**ca. 651** Official version of Koran established **868** The *Diamond Sutra* is printed in China **1413–1416** *Les Très Riches Heures du Duc de Berry*, an illuminated book of hours **ca. 1438** Johannes Gutenberg invents the printing press	**1462** First Frankfurt Book Fair **1464–1483** Printing presses established in Italy, Switzerland, France, the Netherlands, Spain, Hungary, England, and Sweden **1501** Aldus Manutius, founder of the Aldine Press in Venice, Italy, uses italic type for the first time
Arts	**ca. 60,000 B.C.** First flutes, made out of bone **ca. 15,000 B.C.** Lascaux cave paintings **ca. 450 B.C.** Birth of Greek theater	**1026** Guido d'Arezzo names the musical notes (do, re, mi, etc.) **1100s** The troubadour tradition of secular songs and poems develops in southern France **ca. 1440–1450** Fra Angelico's *The Annunciation*	**1500s** Major and minor scales are developed **1523–1526** Albrecht Dürer's *The Four Apostles* **ca. 1550** First performances of the commedia dell'arte in Italy **1572** Andrea Amati makes the first violoncello
Literature	**ca. 3250 B.C.** Invention of writing **1100 B.C.** Pa-out-She, Chinese scholar, compiles first dictionary **ca. 1000 B.C.** Oldest books of the Old Testament are written down **ca. 800 B.C.** Homer's *Iliad* and *Odyssey*	**701–762** Li Po, Chinese poet **ca. 1000** *Beowulf* **ca. 1308–1321** Dante's *The Divine Comedy* **1387–1400** Geoffrey Chaucer's *The Canterbury Tales*	**1532–1534** François Rabelais's *Gargantua and Pantagruel* **1590–1596** Edmund Spenser's *The Faerie Queen* **1594–1595** William Shakespeare's *Romeo and Juliet*
Science	**1.8 million years ago** First stone tools **500,000 B.C.** Taming of fire **10,000 B.C.** Ice Age ends **ca. 3500 B.C.** First known use of wheels in Sumeria **1800 B.C.** Babylonians invent multiplication tables **A.D. 79** Mount Vesuvius erupts and buries Pompeii	**ca. 500** Mathematicians in India invent the zero and decimal numbers **1030** First school of medicine established in Salerno, Italy	**1510–1590** Ambroise Paré, father of modern surgery **1543** Death of Nicolaus Copernicus **1590** Compound microscope invented
History	**1361–1352 B.C.** Egyptian boy king Tutankhamen reigns **ca. 500 B.C.** Buddhism founded **ca. 6 B.C.–A.D. 30** Jesus Christ	**476** Fall of the Roman Empire **ca. 600** Islam religion founded in Arabia **1325** Tenochtitlán, capital of the Aztec empire, founded	**late 1400s** Incas build walled city of Machu Picchu **1492** Christopher Columbus lands in the Bahamas **1517** Martin Luther's Reformation begins

17th Century	18th Century	19th Century	20th Century

1600s Shakespeare's works are published for the first time
1638 Puritans set up first printing press in the United States, in Cambridge, Massachusetts
1640 First book published in colonial America is *The Whole Booke of Psalmes*

1737 Pierre-Simon Fournier develops point system of type measurement
1790 United States adopts first copyright legislation
1792 Founding of first U.S. publishing company, J. B. Lippincott & Co.

1800s The Industrial Revolution brings about technological advances in printing
1800 The Library of Congress is founded in Washington, D.C.
1884 Ottmar Mergenthaler patents first Linotype typesetting machine

1919 U.S. publisher Macmillan and Company institutes a children's department
1926 Book-of-the-Month Club begins distributing new books by mail
1993 Approximately 2,072 billion books are sold in the United States

---

ca. 1600 Japanese develop Kabuki theater
1644–1737 Antonio Stradivari, considered maker of finest violins
1666 Jan Vermeer's *The Letter*

ca. 1708 Johann Sebastian Bach's *Toccata and Fugue in D minor*
1725 Antonio Vivaldi's *The Four Seasons*
1765 John Singleton Copley's *Boy with a Squirrel*

1820s Katsushika Hokusai's *Great Wave off Kanagawa*
1874 Modest Petrovich Mussorgsky's *Pictures at an Exhibition*
1892 Pyotr Ilich Tchaikovsky's *The Nutcracker*

ca. 1900 Birth of jazz
1917–1918 Pablo Picasso's *Woman with a Book*
1939 *The Wizard of Oz*
1955 The beginnings of rock and roll
1981 MTV premieres on cable TV

1611 John Donne's *An Anatomie of the World*
ca. 1612–1672 Anne Bradstreet, Early American poet
1668–1694 Jean de La Fontaine's *Fables*

1700s Tsao Chan's *The Story of the Stone* (greatest Chinese novel)
1719 Daniel Defoe's *Robinson Crusoe*
1726 Jonathan Swift's *Gulliver's Travels*
1751–1772 Denis Diderot's *Encyclopédie*

1850 Nathaniel Hawthorne's *The Scarlet Letter*
1865 Lewis Carroll's *Alice's Adventures in Wonderland*
1884 Mark Twain's *The Adventures of Huckleberry Finn*
1894 Rudyard Kipling's *The Jungle Book*

1910 Frances Hodgson Burnett's *The Secret Garden*
1935 Laura Ingalls Wilder's *Little House on the Prairie*
1950–1956 C. S. Lewis's *Chronicles of Narnia*
1952 E. B. White's *Charlotte's Web*

1609 Galileo constructs first of his many telescopes
1663 Nicolaus Steno demonstrates that the heart is a muscle

1735 Carolus Linnaeus invents a classification system for animals and plants
1743–1794 Antoine-Laurent Lavoisier, the founder of modern chemistry
1752 Benjamin Franklin invents the lightning rod
1793 Eli Whitney invents the cotton gin

1844 Samuel F. B. Morse begins first telegraph service
1876 Alexander Graham Bell patents the telephone
1879 Thomas Alva Edison invents the electric lightbulb
1885 Louis Pasteur develops a vaccine against rabies

1905 Albert Einstein formulates the theory of relativity: $E = mc^2$
1928 Sir Alexander Fleming discovers penicillin
1945 First atomic bomb
1948 First computer developed
1950 Color television
1969 Neil Armstrong walks on the moon

1607 English settlers establish Jamestown Colony in Virginia
1620 Pilgrims land in Massachusetts
1682–1725 Czar Peter the Great reigns in Russia

1773 Boston Tea Party
1776 U.S. Declaration of Independence signed
1789–1799 French Revolution

1831 Sir James Clark Ross finds North Magnetic Pole
1846–1847 Irish potato famine
1861–1865 U.S. Civil War
1899–1900 Boxer Rebellion in China

1914–1918 World War I
1917–1922 Russian Revolution
1939–1945 World War II
1945 The birth of the United Nations
1989 Fall of the Berlin Wall

Illustrators

Nicole Baron: 6tl, 6m–7bl, 7tr, 7br
Jean-Philippe Chabot: 25tr
Chaine 45 with the authorization of Smurfit Condat, France: 12tl, 12bl, 13tml, 13tml (sticker), 13m–13tr
Jacques Dayan: 15tl gatefold recto, 15tm gatefold recto, 15tr gatefold recto, 15ml gatefold recto, 15ml gatefold recto (sticker), 23m, 23bl, 23bl (sticker)
Luc Favreau: 11l gatefold recto, 11tl gatefold verso, 11bl gatefold verso, 11br gatefold verso, 25tl, 26tl, 26ml (© Explorer Archives, Paris, France, Photo Kremer), 26bl
Donald Grant: 4tr, 5t die-cut overlay recto, 5t die-cut overlay verso, 5mt, 20b
Anne Gutman: 22–23 (marbleized paper background)
Jean-Marie Kacedan: 13b
Patrice Larue: 4b, 5b die-cut overlay recto, 5b die-cut overlay verso, 5b, 16bl, 17t, 17ml, 17mr
Jacques Lerouge: inside front cover, 31–46
Jean-Marie Poissenot: 14b
Jame's Prunier: 24 die-cut foldout recto and verso, 25 die-cut foldout verso
Jean-Sylvain Roveri: 22tr, 23tl, 23m
Michel Sinier: 18, 19tr, 19bm, 19br
Jean Torton: 2tl, 2ml, 2b, 3tr, 3m, 3mr, 8bl, 9tr
Pierre-Marie Valat: front cover (after an illustration in Book of Wonders), 20tl, 21 acetate overlay, 21
John Wilkinson: 13tl, 16rc
Nicolas Wintz: 17b

Credits

Aratus of Soli, Phaenomena, 10th century, British Library, London, England: 11mr gatefold verso
© Archiv für Kunst und Geschichte, Berlin, Germany: 30
© Asap, Jerusalem, Israel (Photo Garo Nalbandjan): 3bl
Achille Beltrame, Civil War in Spain, 1939, illustration in La Domenica del Corriere/© Dagli Orti, Paris, France: 25mr die-cut foldout recto
Alonso Berruguete, Saint Dominic and the Albigensians (detail), 15th century,

Museo del Prado, Madrid, Spain/© Dagli Orti, Paris, France: 25ml–25l die-cut foldout recto
Biblioteca Universitaria, Bologna, Italy: 8tr
Bibliotheca Wittockiana, Brussels, Belgium/© Lithographie P. Jacquet, Brussels, Belgium: 27 two-part die-cut foldout recto
Bibliothèque de l'Arsenal, Paris, France/Bibliothèque Nationale de France, Paris, France: 28br
Bibliothèque des Art Décoratifs, Paris, France/© Jean-Loup Charmet, Paris, France: 28b
Bibliothèque des Arts Graphiques, Paris, France: 19tl, 19tm
Bibliothèque Nationale de France, Paris, France: 10tl, 11tr gatefold recto, 11tmr gatefold verso, 15tl, 23mr, 24tr
© The Board of Trustees of the National Museums and Galleries on Merseyside, Liverpool, England: 9tr
© British Museum, London, England: 3tl
Jean de Brunhoff, L'Histoire de Babar, Editions Hachette, Paris, France, 1931: 28tr
Edgar Rice Burroughs, Tarzan of the Apes, illustrated by Burne Hogarth, 1914, © 1972 Edgar Rice Burroughs, Inc.: 28tl
Cabala, Mirror of Art and Nature in Alchimia, Augsburg, Germany, 1616/Bibliothèque Nationale de France, Paris, France: 25br
Capital letters from Heures à l'usage de Rome, early 16th century, Château d'Ecouen, Ecouen, France/© Giraudon, Paris, France: 11lc gatefold verso, 11mc gatefold verso
Lewis Carroll, Alice's Adventures in Wonderland, illustrated by Arthur Rackham, William Heinemann, London, England, 1907/© Pierre Pitrou, Paris, France: 29t die-cut overlay verso
George Catlin, Mandan Indian Chief and His Wife (detail), 1857–1869, National Gallery of Art, Washington, DC/Archiv für Kunst und Geschichte, Berlin, Germany: 9bl
Carlo Collodi, Pinocchio, illustrated by

Attilio Mussino, 1935/© Jean-Loup Charmet, Paris, France: 29t die-cut overlay recto
Commentaries on the Apocalypse of Beatus de Liebana, 10th century/© Biblioteca Real, El Escorial, Spain/© Dagli Orti, Paris, France: 10tr
Centre de Recherches sur la Conservation des Documents Graphiques, Paris, France: 8mr, 27tl left two-part die-cut foldout verso, 27ml left two-part die-cut foldout verso
© Edimédia, Paris, France (Photo J. Guillot): 24mtr
Editions des Catalogues Raisonnés, Paris, France: 22tl
Evangéliaire de l'église de Metz, 10th century, Bibliothèque Nationale de France, Paris, France: 11mbr
© Explorer Archives, Paris, France (Photo J. Desmarteau): 14ml, 24br
Galleria Nazionale d'Arte Moderna, Rome, Italy/© Dagli Orti, Paris, France: 15 gatefold verso–15rc
Gallimard, Paris, France (Patrick Léger): 9tl, 20tr, 23tr, 27tr right two-part die-cut foldout verso
Görlitz Bibliothek, Görlitz, Germany, ca. 1775/© Archiv für Kunst und Geschichte, Berlin, Germany: 27
Gregory the Great, Moralia in Job, 1111, Ms. 168, folio 48 verso, Bibliothèque Municipale, Dijon, France: 11tmr
Conrad Guesner, Histoire des animaux, 16th century, Bibliothèque Municipale, Reims, France: 24mbr
Heures de Charles VIII, 1484, Biblioteca Nacional de España, Madrid, Spain: 8tl
Lois Hobart, Main Reading Room, The New York Public Library, New York, NY: 27ml right two-part die-cut foldout verso
Dr. Heinrich Hoffmann, Der Struuwelpeter, 1845, All Rights Reserved: 29tl
Institute for Oriental Studies, Academy of Sciences of Russia, Saint Petersburg, Russia: 7bl
Amhed Karahisari, Calligraphy for Koran/Musée du Louvre, Paris, France (Photo © Jacqueline Hyde): 6br
Rudyard Kipling, Jungle Book, illustrated by Maurice de Becque,

1930/© Jean-Loup Charmet, Paris, France: 29tr
J. LeGrant, Le Livre de bonnes moeurs, 15th century, Musée de Condé, Chantilly, France/© Giraudon, Paris, France: 26br
Liber Floridus, ca. 1448, Musée Condé, Chantilly, France/© Giraudon, Paris, France: 11br gatefold recto
Livre de prières, 15th century, Bibliothèque Municipale, Colmar, France: 11mr
Abu Mansur, Shamsa, 17th century: 6tr–7tl
Rita Marshall, J'aime pas lire, illustrated by Etienne Delessert, 1992, © Etienne Delessert: 29br
Fabien de Mori, © Office de Coopération et d'Information Muséographique, Museum d'Autun, Autun, France: 27tr left two-part die-cut foldout verso, 27tr left two-part die-cut foldout verso (sticker)
Musée de la Poste, Paris, France: 12tr
Musée de l'Homme, Paris, France (negative © D. Ponsard): 9br
Musée de Peinture et de Sculpture, Grenoble, France/© Dagli Orti, Paris, France: 15b gatefold verso
Musée National du Bardo, Le Bardo, Tunisia/© Giraudon, Vanves, France: 3br
Museo di Colantinio, Naples, Italy/© Scala, Florence, Italy: 10bl
Museo Egizio di Torino, Turin, Italy/© Scala, Florence, Italy: 2tr
© Rapho, Paris, France (Photo Roland and Sabrina Michaud): 6tl, 14tl, 27b left two-part die-cut foldout verso
Papeteries Arjomari, Paris, France: 12mr
© Pierre Pitrou, Paris, France: 22br
Private Collection, Paris, France: 27b right two-part die-cut foldout verso
Psautier de Mayence, 1457, © Artephot, Paris, France (Photo Schneiders): 16tl
Paul de Robien, Histoire ancienne et naturelle de la Province de Bretagne, 1753, Bibliothèque Municipale, Rennes, France: 24tl
Sacramentaire de Gelonne, ca 790–795, Bibliothèque Nationale de France, Paris, France: 11tr, 11tr gatefold verso
Antoine de Saint-Exupéry, Le Petit Prince, 1943, © Editions Gallimard,

Paris, France: 29b die-cut overlay verso
Pierre Salmon, Lamentations, 1409, Bibliothèque Nationale de France, Paris, France: 11lc
Maurice Sendak, Where the Wild Things Are, 1963, © Maurice Sendak: 29b die-cut overlay recto
Robert Louis Stevenson, Treasure Island, illustrated by Ralph Steadman, 1984, © Abdner Stein, London, England/© Pierre Pitrou, Paris, France: 29bl
Vercelli, The Gospels for High Holy Days, ca. 1200, © Dagli Orti, Paris, France: 22bl
Vie des Saints, 15th century, Bibliothèque Municipale, Colmar, France: 11br

Acknowledgments

Claude Bourdois, Paris, France.
Mme Cantini and M. Renaud, Bibliothèque des Arts Graphiques, Paris, France.
Hubert Comte, Paris, France.
Caroline Corre, Paris, France.
Alain Devauchelle, Paris, France.
Pierre-Marie Grinwald, Imprimerie Nationale, Paris, France.
M. Jacquy, Paris, France.
Lithographie P. Jacquet, Brussels, Belgium.
Mme Linarthova and M. Macoin, Curators of the Library of Musée National des Arts Asiatiques Guimet, Paris, France.
Frank Loriou and Sybille Monod, Centre de Recherches sur la Conservation des Documents Graphiques, Paris, France.
Professor Yuri A. Petrosyan, Institute for Oriental Studies, Academy of Sciences of Russia, Saint Petersburg, Russia.
Alexandra Rose, New York, NY.
Special thanks to Emmanuelle Coda, Laïk, Isabelle Doubois-Dumée, and Sylvie Goyon for their special assistance.
Thanks to Armand Israël, author and editor of Livres d'art at Editions des Catalogues Raisonnés, Paris, France.

Have you found the right spot for each sticker?

SCHOLASTIC
VOYAGES
OF DISCOVERY ™

Key:

l = left	b = bottom
r = right	m = middle
t = top	c = column